A true and strange discourse of the trauailes of two English pilgrimes what admirable accidents befell them in their iourney towards Ierusalem, Gaza, Grand Cayro, Alexandria, and other places. Written by Henry Timberlake. (1609)

Henry Timberlake

A true and strange discourse of the trauailes of two English pilgrimes what admirable accidents befell them in their iourney towards Ierusalem, Gaza, Grand Cayro, Alexandria, and other places.
True and strange discourse of the travailes of two English pilgrimes.
Timberlake, Henry, d. 1626.
Pages 12 and 14 misnumbered 21 and 41.
Some print show-through, and some pages stained.
[2], 33, [1] p.
London : Printed for Thomas Archer, and are to be sold at his shop in Popes-head-pallace, neere the Royall Exchange, 1609.
STC (2nd ed.) / 24081
English
Reproduction of the original in the University of Illinois (Urbana-Champaign Campus)

Early English Books Online (EEBO) Editions

Imagine holding history in your hands.

Now you can. Digitally preserved and previously accessible only through libraries as Early English Books Online, this rare material is now available in single print editions. Thousands of books written between 1475 and 1700 and ranging from religion to astronomy, medicine to music, can be delivered to your doorstep in individual volumes of high-quality historical reproductions.

We have been compiling these historic treasures for more than 70 years. Long before such a thing as "digital" even existed, ProQuest founder Eugene Power began the noble task of preserving the British Museum's collection on microfilm. He then sought out other rare and endangered titles, providing unparalleled access to these works and collaborating with the world's top academic institutions to make them widely available for the first time. This project furthers that original vision.

These texts have now made the full journey -- from their original printing-press versions available only in rare-book rooms to online library access to new single volumes made possible by the partnership between artifact preservation and modern printing technology. A portion of the proceeds from every book sold supports the libraries and institutions that made this collection possible, and that still work to preserve these invaluable treasures passed down through time.

This is history, traveling through time since the dawn of printing to your own personal library.

Initial Proquest EEBO Print Editions collections include:

Early Literature

This comprehensive collection begins with the famous Elizabethan Era that saw such literary giants as Chaucer, Shakespeare and Marlowe, as well as the introduction of the sonnet. Traveling through Jacobean and Restoration literature, the highlight of this series is the Pollard and Redgrave 1475-1640 selection of the rarest works from the English Renaissance.

Early Documents of World History

This collection combines early English perspectives on world history with documentation of Parliament records, royal decrees and military documents that reveal the delicate balance of Church and State in early English government. For social historians, almanacs and calendars offer insight into daily life of common citizens. This exhaustively complete series presents a thorough picture of history through the English Civil War.

Historical Almanacs

Historically, almanacs served a variety of purposes from the more practical, such as planting and harvesting crops and plotting nautical routes, to predicting the future through the movements of the stars. This collection provides a wide range of consecutive years of "almanacks" and calendars that depict a vast array of everyday life as it was several hundred years ago.

Early History of Astronomy & Space

Humankind has studied the skies for centuries, seeking to find our place in the universe. Some of the most important discoveries in the field of astronomy were made in these texts recorded by ancient stargazers, but almost as impactful were the perspectives of those who considered their discoveries to be heresy. Any independent astronomer will find this an invaluable collection of titles arguing the truth of the cosmic system.

Early History of Industry & Science

Acting as a kind of historical Wall Street, this collection of industry manuals and records explores the thriving industries of construction; textile, especially wool and linen; salt; livestock; and many more.

Early English Wit, Poetry & Satire

The power of literary device was never more in its prime than during this period of history, where a wide array of political and religious satire mocked the status quo and poetry called humankind to transcend the rigors of daily life through love, God or principle. This series comments on historical patterns of the human condition that are still visible today.

Early English Drama & Theatre

This collection needs no introduction, combining the works of some of the greatest canonical writers of all time, including many plays composed for royalty such as Queen Elizabeth I and King Edward VI. In addition, this series includes history and criticism of drama, as well as examinations of technique.

Early History of Travel & Geography

Offering a fascinating view into the perception of the world during the sixteenth and seventeenth centuries, this collection includes accounts of Columbus's discovery of the Americas and encompasses most of the Age of Discovery, during which Europeans and their descendants intensively explored and mapped the world. This series is a wealth of information from some the most groundbreaking explorers.

Early Fables & Fairy Tales

This series includes many translations, some illustrated, of some of the most well-known mythologies of today, including Aesop's Fables and English fairy tales, as well as many Greek, Latin and even Oriental parables and criticism and interpretation on the subject.

Early Documents of Language & Linguistics

The evolution of English and foreign languages is documented in these original texts studying and recording early philology from the study of a variety of languages including Greek, Latin and Chinese, as well as multilingual volumes, to current slang and obscure words. Translations from Latin, Hebrew and Aramaic, grammar treatises and even dictionaries and guides to translation make this collection rich in cultures from around the world.

Early History of the Law

With extensive collections of land tenure and business law "forms" in Great Britain, this is a comprehensive resource for all kinds of early English legal precedents from feudal to constitutional law, Jewish and Jesuit law, laws about public finance to food supply and forestry, and even "immoral conditions." An abundance of law dictionaries, philosophy and history and criticism completes this series.

Early History of Kings, Queens and Royalty

This collection includes debates on the divine right of kings, royal statutes and proclamations, and political ballads and songs as related to a number of English kings and queens, with notable concentrations on foreign rulers King Louis IX and King Louis XIV of France, and King Philip II of Spain. Writings on ancient rulers and royal tradition focus on Scottish and Roman kings, Cleopatra and the Biblical kings Nebuchadnezzar and Solomon.

Early History of Love, Marriage & Sex

Human relationships intrigued and baffled thinkers and writers well before the postmodern age of psychology and self-help. Now readers can access the insights and intricacies of Anglo-Saxon interactions in sex and love, marriage and politics, and the truth that lies somewhere in between action and thought.

Early History of Medicine, Health & Disease

This series includes fascinating studies on the human brain from as early as the 16th century, as well as early studies on the physiological effects of tobacco use. Anatomy texts, medical treatises and wound treatment are also discussed, revealing the exponential development of medical theory and practice over more than two hundred years.

Early History of Logic, Science and Math

The "hard sciences" developed exponentially during the 16th and 17th centuries, both relying upon centuries of tradition and adding to the foundation of modern application, as is evidenced by this extensive collection. This is a rich collection of practical mathematics as applied to business, carpentry and geography as well as explorations of mathematical instruments and arithmetic; logic and logicians such as Aristotle and Socrates; and a number of scientific disciplines from natural history to physics.

Early History of Military, War and Weaponry

Any professional or amateur student of war will thrill at the untold riches in this collection of war theory and practice in the early Western World. The Age of Discovery and Enlightenment was also a time of great political and religious unrest, revealed in accounts of conflicts such as the Wars of the Roses.

Early History of Food

This collection combines the commercial aspects of food handling, preservation and supply to the more specific aspects of canning and preserving, meat carving, brewing beer and even candy-making with fruits and flowers, with a large resource of cookery and recipe books. Not to be forgotten is a "the great eater of Kent," a study in food habits.

Early History of Religion

From the beginning of recorded history we have looked to the heavens for inspiration and guidance. In these early religious documents, sermons, and pamphlets, we see the spiritual impact on the lives of both royalty and the commoner. We also get insights into a clergy that was growing ever more powerful as a political force. This is one of the world's largest collections of religious works of this type, revealing much about our interpretation of the modern church and spirituality.

Early Social Customs

Social customs, human interaction and leisure are the driving force of any culture. These unique and quirky works give us a glimpse of interesting aspects of day-to-day life as it existed in an earlier time. With books on games, sports, traditions, festivals, and hobbies it is one of the most fascinating collections in the series.

The BiblioLife Network

This project was made possible in part by the BiblioLife Network (BLN), a project aimed at addressing some of the huge challenges facing book preservationists around the world. The BLN includes libraries, library networks, archives, subject matter experts, online communities and library service providers. We believe every book ever published should be available as a high-quality print reproduction; printed on-demand anywhere in the world. This insures the ongoing accessibility of the content and helps generate sustainable revenue for the libraries and organizations that work to preserve these important materials.

The following book is in the "public domain" and represents an authentic reproduction of the text as printed by the original publisher. While we have attempted to accurately maintain the integrity of the original work, there are sometimes problems with the original work or the micro-film from which the books were digitized. This can result in minor errors in reproduction. Possible imperfections include missing and blurred pages, poor pictures, markings and other reproduction issues beyond our control. Because this work is culturally important, we have made it available as part of our commitment to protecting, preserving, and promoting the world's literature.

GUIDE TO FOLD-OUTS MAPS and OVERSIZED IMAGES

The book you are reading was digitized from microfilm captured over the past thirty to forty years. Years after the creation of the original microfilm, the book was converted to digital files and made available in an online database.

In an online database, page images do not need to conform to the size restrictions found in a printed book. When converting these images back into a printed bound book, the page sizes are standardized in ways that maintain the detail of the original. For large images, such as fold-out maps, the original page image is split into two or more pages

Guidelines used to determine how to split the page image follows:

- Some images are split vertically; large images require vertical and horizontal splits.
- For horizontal splits, the content is split left to right.
- For vertical splits, the content is split from top to bottom.
- For both vertical and horizontal splits, the image is processed from top left to bottom right.

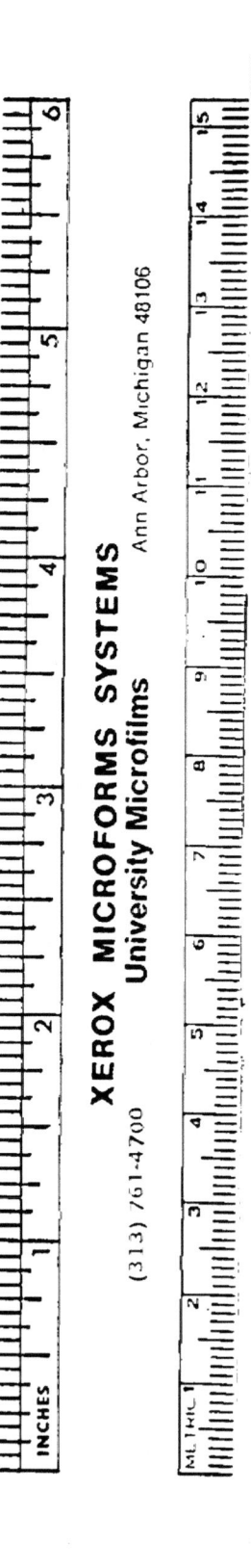

A TRVE AND strange Discourse of

the Trauailes of two English Pilgrimes: what admirable accidents befell them in their iourney towards *Ierusalem, Gaza, Grand Cayro, Alexandria*, and other places.

Also what rare Antiquities, Monuments, and notable memories (according with the auncient remembrances in the holy Scriptures) they saw in *Terra Sancta*: with a perfect discription of the old and new *Ierusalem*, and scituation of the Countries about them.

A discourse of no lesse admiration, then well worth the regarding: written by *Henry Timberlake* on the behalfe of himselfe and his fellow Pilgrime.

LONDON,
Printed for *Thomas Archer*, and are to be sold at his Shop in Popes-head-Pallace, neere the Royall Exchange, 1609.

A true and strange discourse of the late trauailes of two English Pilgrimes: what admirable accidents befell them in their iourney to *Ierusalem,* Grand Cayro, Alexandria, &c.

Although it passe as a generall prouerbe, that trauailers may tell leasings by authoritie, yet I being no way daunted by that bug-beare-thunderbolt, but confidently standing on the iustice of my cause, my kinde commendations to all you my deare friends first remembred, thus from Ierusalem I beginnne to salute you. You shall vnderstand that since my departure from Grand Cayro towardes the Holy land I wrote you a letter from Rama (This Rama is the place where the voice was heard of Rachell, weeping for her children) wherein I certified you of all my proceedings, from Grand Cayro euen to that very place. I sent it with seauen others Letters beside to Damasco in a Carauan, from thence to be conuaide to Constantinople: but doubting least the sayd packet is not as yet come to your handes, I thought it good to write againe vnto you, concerning all my aforesaid proceedings, as also the rest of my voaige to Ierusalem, with my imprisonment and troubles in the Cittie, and what memorable antiquities I saw there and else where, vntill my returne backe to Alexandria: First you shall knowe that I departed not from Grand Cayro till the ninth of March; vppon which day I came to the place

A 3 where

where (it is sayd) the Virgine Marie did stay with our Sauiour Christ. So farre was I accompanied by Anthony Thorpe, and some others that went to Grand Cayro with me, but there left me, departing backe to the Cittie, and I with my fellow trauailer M. Iohn Burrell, both of vs being in our Pilgrims habits came that night to a Towne called Canko, where we were glad to take vp our lodging in a yard, hauing no other bedding then the bare ground. The next day we departed thence, and came to a Towne in the Land of Gozan, where we met with a company of Turkes, Iewes, and Christians, and some 750. Camelles, all which were bound for Damasco ouer the deserts: yet was there amongst them two and twenty Greeks and Armenians, whose purposed trauails lay to Ierusalem, which made vs the gladder of their company. At this Towne, being named Philbits, we staied two dayes and one night: in which time I went into a house, where I saw a very strange secret of hatching Chickines, by artificiall heat or warmth: the like I had seene before at Grand Cayro, but not in such extraordinarie numbers or multitudes as heere: the manner whereof I will declare as followeth. The country People inhabiting about this towne, foure or fiue miles distance euery way, bring their Egges in apt cariage for the purpose, vppon Asses or Camels to this place where there is an Ouen or Furnace purposely kept temperately warme, and the Furner or Maister thereof standeth ready at a little doore to receiue the Egges of euery one, by tale, vnles that when thy number ariseth so high (as to 10. Camels lading or more) then he filleth a measure, by tale, and after that order measures all the rest. And I tell you this for a truth, that I saw there receiued by the Furner, Cooke, or Baker, in one day by tale and by measure, the number of thirty fiue or forty thousand Egges : and they told me, that for three dayes space together, he doeth nothing but

still

ſtill receiue in Egges, and at twelue dayes end they come againe to fetch Chickins, ſometimes at ten dayes, and ſometimes (but not very often) at ſeuen dayes, accoꝛding as the weather falleth out. Perhaps ſome two hundꝛed perſons are owners of one Raungefull, ſome hauing 200. ſome one, oꝛ moꝛe oꝛ leſſe; as the quantities amount to: the Furner noteth the names and poꝛtions of euery bꝛinger, and if he chanceth to haue a hundꝛed and fiftie thouſand, oꝛ two hundꝛed thouſand at one heate (as many times it chanceth that hœ hath) yet doth hee mingle them all together, not reſpecting to whome they ſeuerally belong. Then he laieth them one by one vpon his Raunge, ſo nære as they can lye and touch each other, hauing firſt made a bed foꝛ them of Camels dung burnt: and the place whereon the aſhes doth reſt, is of a very thinne matter made of earth, but mixed with the Camels dung in the making, and ſome Pigeons dung amongſt it: yet herein conſiſteth not the ſecret onely: foꝛ there is a concaue oꝛ hollow place about thꝛe foot bꝛeadth vnder it, whereon is likewiſe ſpꝛead another layer of Camels dung, and vnder that is the place where the fier is made. Yet can I not rightly call it fire, becauſe it appeareth to be nothing but embers: foꝛ I could not diſcerne it but to be like aſhes, yœlding a temperate heate to the next concaue, and the heate being reſiſted by the layer of dung next it (which dung being greene, and laid vpon pæces of withered træs, oꝛ rather boughes of old dead træs) deliuereth foꝛth an extraoꝛdinary vapour, and that vapour entreth the hollow concaue next vnder the Egges, where in time it pærcheth the afoꝛeſaid mixed earth, which toucheth the aſhes whereon the Egges are layde, and ſo ſerueth as a neceſſarie receptacle foꝛ all the heate comming from vnderneath. This artificiall heate glyding thꝛough the embers, whereon the Egges lye, doth by degrœs warme thꝛough the ſhelles, and ſo infuſeth life by the ſame pꝛopoꝛtions of heate: thus in
ſeauen,

seauen, eight, nine, ten, oꝛ sometimes twelue dayes, life continueth by this artificiall meanes. Now when the Furner perceiueth life to appeare, and that the shelles begin to bꝛeake, then he beginneth to gather them: but of a hundꝛeth thousand, he hardly gathereth thꝛee score thousand, sometime but fifty thousand, and sometime (when the day is ouercast) not twenty thousand: and if there chance any lightning, thunder oꝛ raine, then of a thousand he gathers not one, foꝛ then they all miscarry and die. And this is to be remembꝛed withall, that be the weather neuer so fayꝛe, the aire perfect, cleare, and euery thinge as themselues can desire, and let the Chickins be hatched in the best manner that may be, yet haue they either a Claw to much oꝛ to little: foꝛ sometimes they haue fiue Claws, sometimes sixe, some but two befoꝛe, and one behind, and sildome very few oꝛ any in their right shape. Afterwards when the People come to receiue their Egges that befoꝛe had bꝛought them in, the Furner giues to euery one ratably, accoꝛding as the Furnace yeeldeth, reseruing to himselfe the tenth foꝛ his labour. Thus haue you the secret of hatching Chickins by heat artificiall, at the towne of Philbits in the land of Gozan, which I thinke were in vaine to be pꝛactised in England, because the aire there is hardly ten daies together clarified, neither is there any Camels dung, though they haue dung of other beasts euery way as hot: therefoꝛe when the Sunne is in Cancer, Leo, oꝛ Virgo, you may if you please trie what may be done. Perhaps some will thinke this to be a lye oꝛ fable, but to such I answeare, I can vrge their credence no further then my faith and truth may perswade them: and if thereon they will not beléeue me, let them take paines to make their owne eyes a witnes, and when they haue payd as déerely as I haue done (foꝛ the sight of this and other things cost me an hundꝛed Marks in fifty daies) their iudgments will be better confirmed.

But

But now to my iourney toward the desart of Arabia, which I was of force to passe before I could come to the Holy land. Then we departed from the Towne Philbits, trauelling all night in company with the Carauan of Damasco, and the fourtæenth at nine of the clocke, we pitched our tents at Baharo in the land of Gozan. From thence we daparted that night; and the 15. at night, we pitched at Salhia, which is to the eastward of the land Gozan, and stands on the borders of the Arabian desarts: there we stayed two daies for feare of the wilde Arabes, and departed thence the seauentæenth. We passed that night ouer a great bridg, vnder which the Salt-water standeth. This water comes out of the Sea from the parts of Damieta, and by mens hands was cut out of that place, some hundred and fifty miles into the maine land, by Ptolomeus King of Egipt, who purposed to bring the Red-sea, and the Mediterian all into one: but when he foresaw, that if hee had gone through with this worke, all his countrie had béene quite drowned, he gaue it ouer, and builded a bridg there to passe ouer. This place parteth Arabia and Ægipt, and no sooner had we past this bridg, but we were set vpon by the wild Arabes, and notwithstanding our great company, (for wée were more then a thousand persons) a Camell loden with Callicoes was taken from vs, foure of our men hurt, and one of them mortally wounded, and the Arabes ran away with ye prey, we being vnable to help it, because it was night.

The next day we pitched by a well of brackish water: but I forgot to tel you that my fellow Pilgrime, M. Iohn Burrell escaped very narrowly in the last nights bickering: there wée rested our selues til thrée of the clock in the afternowne, which they call Lasara; for the Arabians and Ægiptians deuide the day into foure parts: then we departed and pitched the next morning at a castle in the desart called Catga, which is one of the thrée Castels which the Turks keep in the desarts, to defend all trauailers from the wilde Arabes : Therefore there we payd a certaine tare, which was sixty péeces of siluer of two pence a péece value, for each man or boy, and seuenty fiue

péeces

peeces for a Camell laden, and fourtéene for a Mule. Hauing paid this imposition we departed, & pitched againe the nine-téene at another brakish well, from whence setting onward, we pitched the 20. of March at the second Castle called Arris, kept also by the Turks in the said desarts, where our taxe was but twenty péeces of siluer for each passenger, and thirtie for a Camel. From thence we were guided by many Soldiers to the third Castle called Raphael, making one long iourney of twenty foure houres together. Here it is said that the Kings of Egipt and Iudea fought many great battailes: which to me séemed very vnlikely, because there is nothing to reléeue an armie with all, except sand and salt-water

There we paid ten péeces each passenger, and twenty for a Beast, so departing thence the 22. in the morning we pitched at Gaza in Palestine, a goodly fruitefull Countrie, and there we were quited of al ye desarts. In this towne I saw the place where (as they told vs) Sampson puld downe the two Pillars, and slew the Philistines: and suerly it appeares to be the same towne, by reason of the scituation of the countrie: There we paid twenty two péeces for each beast, and ten each passenger. From hence we departed, and pitched at a place called in Arabian Canute, but by the Christians called Bersheba, being vpon the borders of Iudea, where we paid but 2. péeces of siluer each one, and foure for a beast. Departing thence, the 23. in the morning, we pitched our Tents vpon a gréene close vnder the walles of Ramoth in Gilead: there I stayed al that day, and wrote eight letters for England by the forenamed Carauan, which went for Damasco, to be conueyed to Constantinople, and so for England. The next day being the 24. in the morning, I with other Christians, set toward Ierusalem, and the great Carauan went their way for Damasco, but we pitched short that night at a place called in Arabian Cudechelaneb, being 16. miles from Hebron, where the Sepulchre of our father Abraham is, and 5. little miles from Ierusalem. From thence we departed in the morning being our Lady day in Lent, and 9. of the clocke before
noone,

none, I saw the Cittie of Ierusalem, when knéeling downe, and saying the Lords prayer, I gaue God most harty thanks for conducting me thither, to behold so holy a place with mine eyes, whereof I had read so often before. Comming within a furlong of the Gates, I with my companion M. Iohn Burrell, went singing & praising God, till we came to the West-Gate of the Cittie, and there we stayed, because it is not lawfull for a Christian to enter vnadmitted. My companion aduised me to say I was a Gréeke, onely to auoide going to Masse: but I not hauing the Gréeke tongue, refused so to doe, telling him euen at the entrie of the Gate, that I would neither deny my Country nor Religion, whereupon being demanded who we were, Maister Iohn Burrell (answearing in the Gréeke tongue) told them that he was a Gréeke, and I an Englishman. This gaue him admittance to the Gréeke Patriarke, but I was seazed on and cast in prison, before I had stayed a ful houre at the Gate, for the Turkes flatly denied, that they had euer heard either of my Quéene or country, or that she paid them any tribute. The Pater Guardian, who is the defender of all Christian Pilgrimes (and the principall procurer of mine imprisonment, because I did not offer my selfe vnder his protection, but confidently stood to bée rather protected vnder the Turke then the Pope) made the Turke so much my enemie, that I was reputed to be a spy, and so by no meanes could I be released from the dungeon.

Now giue mee fauour to tell you, (how it pleased God that very day) to deliuer me, and graunt mée passe as a protestant, without yéeldnig to any other ceremonie, then cariage of a Waxe-Candle onely, farre beyond mine expectation. Hére let me remember you, that when I stayed at Ramoth in Gilead, where I wrote the eight Letters for England by the Carauan of Damasco, hauing so good leysure, I went to a Fountaine to wash my fowle linnen, and being earnest about my businesse, suddenly there came a More vnto me, who taking my

cloathes

cloathes out of my hands, and calling me by my name, said he would helpe me.

You doubt not but this was some amazement to mee, to heare such a man call me by my name, and in a place so farre distant from my friends, countrie and acquaintance: which he perceiuing, boldly thus spake in the Franke tongue, why Captaine, I hope you haue not forgotten me, for it is not yet forty daies since you set me a land at Alexandria, with ye rest of those passengers you brought from Argier, in your Ship called the Troian: and here is another in this Carauan, whom you likewise brought in company with you, that would not be a little glad to see you. I demanded of him if hee dwelt there: he answered me no, saying that he & his fellow were going in ye Carauan to Damasco (which place they call Sham) and from thence to Beggdatt which we call Babylon, & from thence to Mecha to make a Hudgee, for so they are called when they haue béene at Mecha: moreouer, he told me that he dwelt in the Citie of Fesse in Barbarie.

This man (in my minde) God sent to be the meanes of mine immediate deliuerie. For after I had taken good notice of him, I well remembred that I saw him in my Ship, though one man among 3. hundred is not very redily known: for so many broght I from Argier into those parts of differēt Nations: as Turkes, Moores, Iewes & Christians: I desired this man to bring me to the sight of his other Companiō, (which hauing washed my linnen) he did, & him I knew very redily. These two concluded, that the one of thē would depart thence with the Carauan, and the other goe along with me to Ierusalem, which was the More before remembred: & such kinde care had the Infidel of me, that he would not leaue me vnaccompanied in this strange Land, which I cānot but impute to Gods especiall prouidence for my deliuerance out of prison, or else had I béene left in most miserable case.

When this More saw me thus imprisoned in Ierusalem, my dungeon being right against the Sepulcher of Christ, albeit he wept, yet he bad me be of good comfort, & went to the

Bashawe

Bashawe of the Cittie, and to the Saniacke, before whom hee tooke his oath, that I was a Mariner of a Shippe, which had brought two hundred and fiftie, or three hundred Turkes & Mores into Egipt from Argyer and Tunis, their iourney being vnto Mecha.

This More (in regard he was a Muzzleman) preuailed so well with them, that returning with sir Turkes backe to prison, he called me to the doore and there said vnto me, that if I would go to the house of the Pater Guardian, and yeelde my selfe vnder his protection, I should be inforced to no Religion but mine owne, except it were to carrie a Candle: to the which I willingly condescended.

So paying the charges of the prison, I was presently deliuered and brought to the Guardians Monasterie, where the Pater comming to me, tooke me by the hand and bad me welcome, meruailing I would so much er from Christianity, as to put my selfe rather vnder the Turks then his protection: I told him what I did, was because that I would not goe to Masse, but keepe my conscience to my selfe: He replyed that many Englishmen had beene there, but beeing (Catholiques) went to Masse, telling the Turkes at the Gates entrance that they were Frenchmen, for the Turkes know not what you meane by the word Englishman: aduising me further, that when any of my countrymen vndertooke the like trauaile, at the Gates of Ierusalem, they should tearme themselues either French-men or Brittans, because they are well knowne to the Turkes.

This or such like conference past betweene vs: and further he asked me how old our Queenes Maiestie was, & what was the reason she gaue nothing to the maintenãce of the holy Sepulcher, as well as other Kings and Princes did? with diuerse other friuolous questions, whereto I answered accordingly. This day being spent euen to twi-light, Master Iohn Burrel, who passed for a Greeke without any trouble, came in vnto vs, being neuerthelesse constrained to this Monastery, or else he might not stay in the Cittie: for such sway do ẙ Papists

pists carry there, that no Christian stranger can haue admittance there, but he must be protected vnder them, or not enter the citie. Maister Burrell and I being together in the court of the Monasterie, twelue fat-fed Friers came forth vnto vs, each of them carying a Wire candle burning, and two spare candles beside, the one for Maister Burrell, the other for me. Another Frier brought a great bason of warme water, mingled with Roses and other sweet flowers, and a Carpet being spread on the ground, and Cushions in Chaires set orderly for vs, the Pater Guardian came & set vs downe, giuing each of vs a Candle in our hands, then came a Frier and puld off our hose, and (setting the Bason on the Carpet) washed our fæte.

So sone as the Frier began to wash, the twelue Friers began to sing, continuing so till our fæt were washed; which being done, they went along singing, and we with the Guardian came to a chappel in the Monasterie, where one of them began an Oration in forme of a sermon, tending to this effect, how meritorious it was for vs to visite the Holy land, and see those sanctified places where our Sauiours fæte had strode.

The Sermon being ended, they brought vs vnto a chamber where our supper was prepared, there we fed somwhat fearfully, in regard that strange cates haue as strange qualities: but committing our selues to God, and their outward appearing Christian kindenesse, we fell to hartily, supt very bountifully, and after (praising God) were lodged decently. Thus much for my first entertainment in Ierusalem, which was the 25. day of March 1601. being our Lady day in Lent. Now followes what the Friers afterward shewed me, being thereto appointed by the Pater Guardian. Early the next morning we arose, & hauing saluted ye Pater Guardian, he appointed vs seauen Friers and a Truochman: so forth we went to see all the holy places in the citie which were to be seen, except those in Sepulchra Sancta: for that required a whole dayes worke afterward, and at euery place where we came we knæeled

led downe, and saide the Lords prayer.

The first place of note that the Friers shewed vs, was the place Iudicial next the house of Veronica Sancta: & demaunding of them what Saint that was, they told me it was she that did wipe our Sauiours face, as he passed by in his agonie.

Descending a little lower in the same stréete, they shewed me the way whichour Sauiour Christ went to crucifiing, called by them Via Dolorosa.

Then on the right hand in the same stréete, I was showen the house of the rich glutton, at whose gate poore despised Lazarus lay.

Holding on our way downe this stréete, we came to a turning passage on the left hand, whence they told me Simon Sirenus was comming toward the Dolorous way, when the Souldiers seeing him, called him, and compelled him, against his will, to helpe our Sauiour to carry his Crosse

Then they told me, that in that same place the People wept, when Christ answearing, said vnto them, Oh Daughters of Ierusalem weepe not for me,&c.

Next they shewed me the Church where the Virgin Marie fell into an agonie, when Christ passed by carying his Crosse.

Afterward they brought me to Pilates Pallace, which though it be all ruinated, yet is there an old Arch of stone, which is still maintained by the Christians, and it standing ful in the high way, we passed vnder it: much like the way of passage vnder Maister Hammons house in the Bulworke, but that the Arche is higher: for vpon that Arche, is a Gallerie, which admitteth passage (ouer our heades) from one side of the stréete to the other: for Pilates Palace extendeth ouer the high way on both sides, and Pilate had two great windowes in the said Gallerie, to gaze out both wayes into the stréete, as Maister Hammon hath the like aduantage at both his windowes.

Into

Into this Gallerie, was our Sauiour brought when hée was showen vnto the Iewes, and they standing below in the stréete, hard the words, Ecce Homo. A little from this place, is y̑ foot of the staires, where our Sauiour did first take vp his Crosse. Then they brought me to the place where the Virgin Marie was conceiued & borne, which is the Church of Saint Anna, and no turkish Church. Next, they shewed me the pole, where Christ clensed the Leapers, and then guiding me to Saint Stephens gate a little without it vpon the left hand, they shewed me the stone wheron Saint Stephen was stoned. From hence I saw the staires going vp to port Area, at which port there are diuers Reliques to be séene, it was the East gate of the Temple which Salomon built vpon mount Moria, in which Temple was the place of Sanctum Sanctorum, but now in that place is builded a goodly great Church, belonging to the Turkes.

Thus spent I the second day, being the 26 day of March: All within the gates of Ieru∫alem except my going to sée the stone wherewith Saint Stephen was stoned. The next day being the 27. hauing done our dutie to God, and the Pater Guardian, we hired Asses for the Friers and the Trouchman to ride on, and going forth the Cittie gates, we mounted and rode directly toward Bythinea.

By the way as we rode, they shewed me the place of the fruitlesse Fig-trée, which Christ cursed: next, the Castle of Lazarus, that Lazarus whom Christ loued so well: for his house or Castel was in Bythinea, but it was vtterly ruinated and nothing to be séene but the two sides of the wall.

In the same Towne, they shewed me the house of Mary Magdalen, but so ruinated, that nothing is left of it but a péece of a wal, there I saw likewise Marthaes house consisting of 2. péeces of a wal: & thence they brought me to y̑ stone where the two sisters told Christ, that Lazarus was dead, from wence passing on, they shewed me the place where our Sauiour rai∫ed Lazarus from death, after he had lyen thrée daies in the ground, and where he was buried afterward when hée dyed.

This

This place hath bene notably kept from the beginning, and is repaired still by the Christians: but yet in poore and verie bare sort: And this is all that I saw in Bythinea.

From hence we rode vnto Mount Oliuer, and passing by Bethphage, they brought me to ye place where our Sauiour tooke the Asse and Colt, when he rode to Ierusalem vpon Palme-sunday. Riding from Bethphage directly North, we came to the fot of Mount Oliuer, where they shewed mée the place Benedicta of the Virgin Maries Annunciation: ascending to the top of the mount, we saw the place of our Sauiours Ascention: at the sight whereof we said our prayers, and were commaunded withal to say fiue Pater Nosters and fiue Aue Maries, but we said the Lords prayer, tooke notice of the place and departed. This is the very highest part of Mount Oliuer, and hence may bée descerned many notable places: as first West from it, is the prospect of the new Citie of Ierusalem: Southwest from it may be séen ye prospect of Mount Syon, which is adioyning to new Ierusalem: also in the valley betwéene Syon and the Mount whereon I stwd, I saw the brooke Cedron, the Poole Silo, the Garden wherin our Sauiour prayed, the place where afterward hée was betrayed, and diuers other notable thinges in this valley of Gethsemanie: as the Tomb of Absolon, King Dauids Son, the Tomb of Iehoshaphat, and others which I wil speake of when I come to them.

Ful South from Mount Oliuer I could sée the places we came last from, as all Bythinea & Bethphage: also east northeast from this mount, may be séen both the Riuer of Iordan, which is some fiftéen miles off, and Iericho, which is not far, because it is to the Westward of Iordan.

From Mount Oliuer East and East South-east, may be séene the lake of Sodome and Comorrha, which is some hundred miles long, and eight miles ouer: all these places I set with the compasse, when I was on Mount Oliuer: for I stayed on the top of it some two houres and a halfe, hauing a little Compasse about me.

C   Descending

Descending hence toward the foote westward, we came to a place where the Friers told me, that a Woman called Saint Pelagia did pennance in the habit of a Frier: whereat I smiling, they demaunded why I did so? I answered that to beleeue Pelagia was a Saint, stood out of the Compasse of my Creede: they told me, when I should come home at night they would shew me sufficient Authors for it: but whē I came home I had so much to do in writing my notes out of my table book, that I had not leysure to vrge their Authors for Saint Pelagia.

By this time they brought vs to the place where our Sauiour did fore-see the iudgement, then where he made the Pater Noster, and then where the Apostles made the Creede.

From hence we came to the place where Christ wept for Ierusalem, and from thence to the place where the Virgin Mary gaue the Girdle to Saint Thomas: and then to the place where she prayed for Saint Stephen: al these last were comming downe Mount Oliuer toward the valley of Gethsemanie, where by the way we came to our Ladies Church, wherein is her Sepulcher, & the Sepulcher of her Husband Ioseph, with the Sepulcher of Anna, and many others in that Church.

This Church standeth at the foote of Mount Oliuer, and was built (as they say) by Helena the Mother of Constantine the great: here the Friers went into the Virgin Maries Sepulcher, & there either said Masse or Prayers, while wee in the meane time went to dinner.

In this Church is a Fountaine of excéeding fine water, and in regard we went downe into a Vault as it were, it giueth a meruailous lowd Ecchs or sound.

Hence went we to the Caue, whither Iudas came to betray Christ, when he was at Prayer, and thence to the Garden where our Sauiour left his Disciples, commaunding them to watch and pray, but found them sleeping at his returne: then they brought me to the Garden where Christ was taken, and all these last three were in the valley of
Gethsemany,

Gethsemany.

Riding vnto the towne,(whereof the valley beares name) on the left hand I saw the before remembred Sepulchers of Absolon and Iehoshaphat, and on the right hand the brooke Cedron, which at my being there had not one drop of water in it, (for indéed) it is but a ditch to conuey the water from the two hilles,(I meane Mount Oliuet and Mount Syon) when any store of raine falleth. And this ditch or brooke Cedron is in the valley betwéene both those hilles.

Hard by the brooke Cedron, they shewed me a stone marked with the féete and elbowes of Christ, in their throwing of him downe when as they tooke him, and euer since (say they) haue those prints remained there.

From thence we rode to the place where Saint Iames the younger did hide himselfe, and afterward was buried there: there also they shewed where Zachariah the son of Barachiah was buried, and brought me to another place, where (they say) the Virgin Marie vsed often to pray.

Then came we often to the poole of Silo, wherin M. Burrel & I washed our selues, and hence we were showen the place where the Prophet Esay was sawen in péeces: thence they guiding vs to an excéeding déepe well, where the Iewes (as they say) hide the holy fire in the time of Nabuchodonozer.

Here we ascended from the valley to a hil side, which lyeth iust South frō Mount Syon, but there is a great valley betwéene, called Gehemion, and there they shewed me the place where the Apostles hid themselues, being a Caue in a Rocke. Ascending higher hence, they brought me to ỹ field, or rather to be more rightly termed the Rocke, where the common buriall place is for strangers, being the very same (as they say) which was bought with ỹ 30. péeces of siluer, that Iudas receiued as the price of his Maister, which place is called Aceldoma, and is fashioned as folloeth. It hath 3. holes aboue, & on the side there is a vent, at the vpper holes they vse to let down ỹ dead bodies, to the estimation of some fifty foote downe.

In this place I saw two bodies, new or very lately let downe, and looking downe (for by reason of the three great holes aboue, where the dead bodies lye, it is very light) I receiued such a sauor into my head, as it made me very sick, so that I was glad to entreate the Friers to goe no further, but to returne home to the Citie.

So here we went through the valley of Gehemion, and at the foote of Mount Syon (hauing a little bottle of water, which I brought from the Poole Silo) I dranke, and rested there an houres space, eating a few Raisons and Oliues, which wee brought with vs from Ierusalem in the morning.

After I had well rested and refreshed my selfe, we began to ascend Mout Syon, and a little way vp the hil they shewed me the place where Peter hauing denyed Christ, and hearing the Cocke crow, went out and wept.

Ascending higher, they shewed me the house where the Virgin Mary dwelt, which was neere vnto the Temple: then they brought me to the place, where the Iewes setting on the blessed Virgin Mary to take her, she was conuaied away by miracle.

Hence we went to the house of Caiphas, which was somewhat higher vpon Mount Syon, and there I saw the prison wherein our Sauiour was detained. Passing on still higher, they guided me to a little Chappell which is kept by the Armenians, whereinto entring, at the high Alter they shewed me the stone which was vpon our Sauiours Sepulcher (as they say) & it is neer to y place where Peter denied Christ: for there they shewed me the Pillar whereon the Cock stood when he crowed.

Hence was I brought to the place where our Sauiour made his last Supper, and thence I came where the holy Ghost descended vpon the Apostles: whence passing on, they shewed me the place where Christ appeared to his Disciples the eight day after his Resurrection, when Saint Thomas desired to see his woundes.

Neere

Néere to this place vpon Mount Sion, the virgin Mary dyed, and hard by they shewed me a place bought by the Pope of the Turks, for the buriall of the Europian Christians, because he would not haue them cast into Aceldema: they told vs that the yeare before, fiue Englishmen were buried in y place, whether by the Friers poysoning them, or howsoeuer else it hapened, but we thought it strange that al fiue should die together in one wéeke. Thence came we to the house of Annas the high Priest, which is now but a paire of very old walles, and nothing else of it to be séene: but at the side of one of the walles is an old Oliue trée, whereto they told me that our Sauiour was fast bound: and demaunding a further reason thereof, they said that when he was brought vnto this house, Annas being asléepe, his people would not awake him: so during their time of stay, they bound him to y said Oliue trée, and when he awaked, then he was brought in and examined.

Departing hence toward the South gate of y Citie, which standeth likewise vpon Mount Sion, we alighted from our Asses, and entring, I noted it well: for now I had séen thrée of the foure gates.

And being desirous to sée the North gate also, they brought me to the Church of S. Thomas, which is within the wal al ruinated: thé to the Church of S. Mark, whether Peter came being deliuered out of prison by the Angell that brake open the gate. Thé they shewed me y house of Zebedeus, whence we came to a place kept by the Abashenes, and there ascending first by a dark way, led on by a liñe or cord, we attained to a high place néere to the Sepulchra Sancta, where I paide two péeces of siluer to go in, and being entred, I demaunded what place it was? the same (quoth they) where Abraham would haue sacrificed his sonne Isaac.

Thence went we to the prison where Saint Peter & Saint Iohn were, being the next dore to the prison wherin I was put before: which made me the sorrier, yit was not my fortune

tune to haue gone into it being so néere it.

Hence we came to the North-gate being on Mount Caluarie side, where hauing well viewed the gate, and perceiuing it waxed late, we went directly home : this was my third dayes worke, in & about Ierusalem, wearied not a little with often alighting to pray: for at each seueral place before recounted, we dismounted and said the Lords prayer on our knées.

On the morrow being the 28. early in the morning, we tok our Asses, riding forth at the West gate, through which I first entred, and passing on the South-ward, we left Mount Sion on the left hand: at the foot whereof they shewed me the house of Vriah, and the Fountaine where Bersaba washed her selfe, when King Dauid espied her out of his Terret.

Thence went we to the place where the Angell toke vp Abacuck by the haire of the head, to carrie meat to Daniell in the Lions denne. Next came we to the place where the wiseman found the Starre when it was lost, & then where the Uirgin Marie rested her selfe vnder a trée, as she came from Bethelem to Ierusalem, which trée they still repaire by setting another close to the rote of it.

Hence rode we to the house of Elias the Prophet, where they shewed me his vsual place of sléeping, & this house standeth so vpon a hil, as from thence I did sée Bethlem a far off.

Thence we went to an old ruinated house, which they told me was Iacobs: which may the better appeare to be so, for in the field thereto adioyning, is the tombe of Rachell Iacobs wife: and some two miles from this tomb is a towne in the same field called Bethesula, the inhabitants whereof are all Christians

In this great field (being betwéene Ierusalem and Bethlem) did lye the Camp of Senacherib when he besieged Ierusalem. From hence we rode to the field, where the Angels brought tydings of great ioy to the Shepheards, which is two miles from Bethlem: and thence we rode to Bethlem

to

to the Monasterie, wherin were some ten Friers: who welcommed me very kindely, and brought me first into a great Church, then into a large entrie, wherein I saw the name of Maister Hugo Stapers twise set, one aboue another, and betwéene them both I set my name.

Then they guided me down the staires into a vault, where was a Chappell set in the place of our Sauiours Natiuity, enclosing both it, and the Maunger wherein Christ was laide, and also the place where he was presented with gifts by the Wise men.

Ouer this Chappell is a great Church, built by Quéene Helena Mother to Constantine the great (as they say) and further I saw diuers Tombs of holy men and others.

Going vp to the top of the Church, I saw vpon the leads the name of Maister Hugo Stapers againe ingrauen, which made me looke the earnestlyer for some other Englishmens names: but finding none, I graued downe my name and came away; then went we in and dined with the Friers.

After dinner, they brought me to the place where the virgine Marie hid her-selfe, when search was made to kill the Children.

So taking my leaue of Bethlem, giuing the Friers thrée péeces of gold, for my dinner and my company withme, béeing eight in number, mounting on our Asses, we rode to the Well, where King Dauids thrée Captaines fetched water for him, through the whole hoste of the Philistines: which standeth a little way from Bethlem, towards Ierusalem, and hath thrée places to draw water vp.

Hence went we presently backe to Ierusalem, entring the gate at foure of the clocke in the afternowne; and at fiue, the Turks let vs in to the Sepulchra Sancta, each of vs paying nine péeces of gold for our entrance.

No sooner were we in, but they locked the gates, so there I stayed til eleuen of the clocke the next day, and then came we forth: now followes what I saw in Sepulchra Sancta,

First

20

First I noted hanging without the gate, at the least a hundred lines or strings, and in the gate is a great hole, whereat a little child may easily creepe in: whereof demaunding the reason they told me ye the hole serued to giue victuals at, for thē which lye within the Church, which are aboue three hundred persons, men and women al Christians, and there they liue continually night and day, and can haue no passage in nor out, but when the Turkes do open the gate for some Pilgrime: which hapeneth not sometims in fourtéene dayes: wherfore these Christian leigers in the Church haue there their whole houshold, and boorded lodgings there builded for them.

The strings before spoken of hanging at the gate, haue each one a Bel fastened at the lodgings, and when their seruants (which are without) bring them any meat, each rings the Bell belonging to his houshold, and so come accordingly (each knowing their owne Bell) for receipt of their foode.

The seueral sorts of Christians which I saw in this Church I will in order describe vnto you.

First the Romaines, for they bare the greatest sway of all. Secondly, the Greekes, for they are next in Number to the Romaines, yet litle better thē slaues to the Turke. Thirdly the Armenians, who haue bin so long time seruants to the Turk, that hauing forgotten their own Language, they vse all their cerimoniés in the Arabian tongue, and so I heard them. The fourth sort of Christians are Nestorians, who are as slaues to the Turke, and haue no other Language thē the Arabian. The fift are the Abashenes, being people of the land of Prestor Iohn. The sixt are the Iacobines that are circumcised Christians, but slaues likewise & seruants to ye Turke.

All these (Christians in name) haue bought of the Turke their seuerall places in this Church, and by-roomes for ease, being neuer fewer in number of al these sir sortes then two hundred & fifty or three hundred continually there lying, and praying after their manner.

The places where they ordinarily vse to go and say their
deuotions

deuotions are thus as I describe them, and as the Romane Friers brought me to them.

First the Piller whereat our Sauiour was whipped. Secōdly ý place where he was impꝛisoned, while they wers pꝛeparing oꝛ making his Croſſe. Thirdly where the Souldiers diuided his Garments. Fourthly where the Croſſe was found by Quéene Helena, which is at the fote of Mount Caluarie, and hard by it is the Chappel of of the said Quéene Helena. Fiftly, the place wherᵉ Chꝛiſt was crowned with thoꝛnes: which I could not ſée til I was glad to giue the Abaſhenes that kept it two péeces of ſiluer. Sixtly the place where the Croſſe being laide along on the ground, our Sauiour was nailed faſt vnto it.

Seauenthly the place on the top of Mount Caluarie, where the Croſſe ſtod when as he ſuffered. Eightly, ý Rocke that rent at his crucifying, which is a thing wel woꝛth the beholding, foꝛ it is ſlit like as it had bin cleft with wedges and Bétles, euen from the top to the two third parts downewards, as it were thꝛough the bꝛow and bꝛeſt of the Rocke: noꝛ is the rent ſmal, but ſo great in ſome places, that a man might eaſily hide himſelfe in it, and ſo groweth down-ward leſſe and leſſe.

Ninthly, the place where the thꝛée Maries annointed Chꝛiſt after he was dead. Tenthly, where he appeared to Mary Magdalen in the likeneſſe of a Gardiner: and whence we came to the Sepulcher it ſelf, which is ý laſt place where they vſe any pꝛayers: from whence I went to ſée the Tombes of Baldwin & Godfrey of Bulloigne: and returning thence back to the Sepulcher, I meaſured the diſtance betwéen place and place, ſpending thus the time frō fiue of the clock befoꝛe night when I went in, vntil next day at eleuen of the clock at my comming foꝛth, wꝛiting downe all things which I thought noteworthy.

My compaṇion Maiſter Iohn Burrell and I beeing thus

D

thus come forth of the Church, we went to the Pater Guardians to dinner, where we hard tidings that fiue other Englishmen were arriued at the Cittie gates, directing towards Alepo. Their names were M. William Bedle, preacher to the English marchants, which were Liegers at Alepo: M. Edward Abbot seruant to the right worshipfull sir Iohn Spencer: M. Geffrey Kirbie, seruant to the worshipfull: M. Paule Banning: and Liegers for them in Alepo: two other young men, the one called Iohn Elkins, the other Iasper Tymne. These fiue hearing of my being there, came all to the house, and these (though they saw not mine imprisonment, nor were with me at the sight of those things in and about Ierusalem) can witnesse, that they were acquainted therewith at the gates, and testifie the other truthes beside. These men, as also my companion M. Iohn Burrel, I left behind me in Ierusalem, departing thence to see other places in the Countrie of Palestine: but let me first tel you, what I obserued in the Cities scituation, because I was informed before I came to see it that it was all ruined, (albeit one the sight thereof) I found it otherwise, hauing a little compasse about me, to set such places as I could easily come by.

Understand then first of all, that the very hart of the old Citie was seated on Mount Sion and Mount Moria: to the North part whereof, was Mount Caluaire without the gates of the old Cittie, about a stones cast and no further. But now I find this new citty scituated so farre in the North part, that it is almost quite off mount Sion, but yet not off mount Moria, which was between mount Sion and mount Caluerie, so that now (vndoubtedly) the South wales of the citie, are placed on the north fote of the hill of Syon. The east wall which doth confront Mount Oliuet, is a great parte of the ancient wal, & so from the South-east angle north, a quarter of a mile behinde mount Caluaire: so that

mount

mount Caluarie, which was in former times a stones caste without the cittie, and the apointed place for ordinarie execution, I findit to be now seated in the heart or middle of the new cittie.

This mount Caluarie is not so high as to be called a mount, but rather a piked or aspiring Rock: for I noted the scituation of it, both whē I was at the top of it, and when I came to the Sepulcher: the Sepulcher being distant from it (I meane from the fot of it) 173. fote, as I measured it: whereupon I conclude, that the place of buriall, which Ioseph of Aramathia made for himselfe was from the fote of Mount Caluarie 173. fote westward, in which place is the Sepulcher of our Sauiour.

The Sepulcher it selfe is two fote and a halfe high from the ground, Eight fot in lenght, and foure fote broad wanting thrée inches, being couered with a faire stone of white colour. Ouer the Sepulcher is a Chappell builded, the north wall whereof is ioyned close with the North side of the Sepulcher: and the Chappell is of like stone, as the Sepulcher is, consisting of fiftéene fote in bredth, fiue and twenty fote in length, and aboue forty fote in height. In this Chappell are alwaies burning thirty or forty Lamps, but vppon Festiuall dayes more, Which are maintained by Gifts giuen at the death of Christians in Spaine, Florence, and other partes, to be kept continually burning, and the giuer of these Lampes, haue their names ingrauen about the vpper edges of them, in Letters of Golde standing in a band of gold or siluer.

This Chappell is inclosed with a Church, and yet not it onely, but therewith is cirkeled in, all the before named Holy places, viz. where Christ was whipt: where he was in prison: where his Garments were deuided: where the Crosse was found: where he was crowned with Thornes: where he was nayled on the

D 2 crosse:

crosse: where the crosse stood when he suffered: where the vaile of the Temple rent: where ye three Maries annointed him: where he appeared to Mary Magdalen: & in briefe, al ye most notable things either about mount Caluarie, or Iosephs field of Aramathia: are inclosed within the compasse of this Church, which was builded by ye fore-remembred Queene Helena, Mother to Constantine ye great, she being (as I haue read in some Authors) an Englishwoman, and daughter to King Coel, that builded Colchester: which being vrged to them, they denyed it. I measured this Church within, and found it to be 422. fadomes about: the one side of it likewise I found it to be 130. fadomes: thus much for Mount Caluarie, which is in the middest of the Cittie now.

From the North-east angle of the Citie to the northwest, is the shortest way of the citie, & from the Northwest angle to the South-west, is as farre as from the South-east to the North-east: but from the Southwest to the South-east which is the South-wal that standeth on the fot of Mount Syon, I measured, and found it to be 3775. foote, which is about three quarters of a mile. Upon this South side of the citie, is a great Iron gate, about which gate are laid seuenteene peeces of brasse Ordinance: this gate is as great as the west gate of the Tower of London, and exceeding strong, the wals being very thicke, and on the South side 50. or 60. foote high: so much for the South Wall and side of the Citie.

The North wall is not altgether so long, but much stronger, for on the North side it hath bene often surprised but on the South-side neuer: and one the East side it is impregnable, by reason of the edge of the Hill which it standeth on, which is fiue times as high as the Wall.

On the North side also are 25 peeces of brasse ordináce
neere

néere to the gate, which is of Iron also, but what is in other places, as at ye corners or angles, I could not come to see, and demaund I durst not. The East wall, containing the gate where S. Stephen was stoned, a litle without, and to this day called Saint Stephens gate; I saw but fiue péeces of ordinance there, and they were betwéene the gate and the relique of port Aurea, which is to the Southward: and concerning the West side of the citie, at ye gate wherof I entred at my first arriuall, it is very strong, likewise, and hath fiftéene péeces of Ordinance lying néere together, and all of brasse: This gate is also made of Iron, and this West wall is altogether as long as the East wall. But it standeth vpon the higher ground: so that comming from the West to the West wall, you can sée nothing within the Citie but ye bare wal, but vpon Mount Oliuer, comming towards the Citie from the East, you haue a very goodly prospect of the Citie, by reason the Citie standeth all on the edge of the Hill.

To conclude, this Citie of Ierusalem is the strongest of al the Cities that I haue yet séen in my iouney, since I departed from Grand Cayro: but the rest of the countrie is very easie to be intreated: yet in ye citie of Ierusalem are thrée Christians for on Turke, and many Christians in ye Country round about, but they al liue porely vnder the Turke.

Now concerning how the Countrie about Ierusalem lyeth, for your more easie and perfect vnderstanding, I will familierly compare their seueral places, with some of our natiue English townes and Villages, according to such true estimatiō as I heare made of the. Imagine I begin with London, I meane much vpon the point or distance.

The Citie of Bethlem, where Christ our Sauiour was borne, is from Ierusalem as Wansworth is from London, I meane much vpon the point in distance.

D.3   The

The plaine of Mamre is from Ierusalem, as Guilford is from London: in which place or neere to it, is the citie of Hebron, where our father Abraham lyeth buried.

Beersheba is from Ierusalem, as Alton is from London, Ramoth Gilead is from Ierusalem, as Reading is from London.

Gaza which is the South-west parts of Palestine, is from Ierusalem as Salisburie is from London.

Ascalon is from Gaza North-east.

Ioppe is from Ierusalem, as Albury is from London.

Samaria is from Ierusalem, as Royston is from London

The Citie of Nazareth is from Ierusalem as Norwich is from London.

Frō Nazereth to moūt Tabor & Hermon, is 5. miles North-east: these two do stand very neer together, Tabor, being the greater.

From Tabor to the Sea Tiberias, is eight miles North-east.

From Ierusalem to mount Sania, is ten dayes iourney, and north-east thence.

These places last spoken of (beginning at Samaria) I was not in, but the other fiue Englishmen that met me in Ierusalem, comming through Galilee, they came through them, and of them had this discription: they receiued of me likewise the discription of my iourney through Palestine.

The place where Christ fasted 40 daies & 40 nights, called Quarranto, is from Ierusalem as Chelmesford is from London.

The riuer Iordane (the very neerest part thereof) is from Ierusalem as Epping is from London.

Iericho, the neerest part of the plaine thereof, is from Ierusalem, as Lowton Hall (sir Robert Wraths house) is from London.

The lake of Sodome and Gomoroh, is from Ierusalem as Grauesend is from London.

The

The ruer Iordan runneth into this Lake, and there dyeth, w is one of the greatest secrets (in my minde) in the world, that a fresh water should run continually into this Salt Lake, and haue no issue out, but there dyeth: and the sayd Lake continuing still so salt, as no waight of any reasonable substance wil sink into it, but flœteth vpon it as a dead man or beast will neuer goe downe. And further note, that what filth soeuer is brought into it by y riuer Iorden, or any other substāce, it flœteth continually vpon the water, and being tossed there on by force of the weather in time it becommeth a coniealed froth, which being cast vpon the banks and there dryed by the extreame heat of the Sun, becommeth blacke like pitch, which in that country is called Bitamon, whereof I haue brought some with me from thence. This lake is about 8. or 9. miles broad, & about 80. or 100. miles long the length stretching from the north, where the riuer Iordan falieth into it to the south ward, and hath no further Issue.

The fields where the Angels brought tydings vnto the shepheards, lyeth from Ierusalem, as Greenewich doth from London.

Mount Oliuer lyeth from Ierusalem as Bow from London.

Bethania is from Ierusalem as Blackewall is from London.

Bethage is from Ierusalem as Mile-end is from London.

The valley Gethsemanie, is from Ierusalem, as Ratchliffe fields lie from London.

Brooke Cedron is from Ierusalem as the ditch without Algate is from London.

Mount Syon is nære adioyning to Ierusalem, as Southwarke ioyneth to London.

Thus haue I described the Citie of Ierusalem, as it is now built, with all the notable places therein, and

ners

néere vnto the same, and the country about it, by which comparisons you may well vnderstand the scituation of most parts of the places néere vnto it, and thereby you may perceiue that it was but a small Country, and a very little plot of ground, which the Isralites possessed in the Land of Canaan, which as now is a very barren Country: for that within 15. miles from Ierusalem the country is wholy barren, and full of rocks, and stony, and vnlesse it be about the plaine of Ierico, I know not any part of the country at this present that is fruitfull, what it hath béene in times past, I referre you to the declaration thereof, made in the holy Scriptures: my oppinion is, that when it was fruitfull, and a Land that flowed with Milke and Hony. In those daies God blessed it, and that as then they followed his commaundements, but now being inhabited by Infidels, (that prophane the name of Christ, and liue in all filthy and beastly manner,) God cursseth it, and so it is made barren, : for it is so barren that I could get no bread when I came néere vnto it, for that one night as I lodged short of Ierusalem, at a place called in the Arabian tongue, Cuda Chenaleb, I sent my More to a house (not far from ye place where we had pitched our Tents) to get some bread, & he brought me word that there was no bread there to be had, and that the man of that house did neuer eate bread in all his life, but onely dryed Dates, nor any of his houshold, wherby you may partly perceiue the barrennesse of the Country at this day, onely as I suppose by the cursse that God layeth vpon the same, for that they vse the sin of Sodom and Gomorah very much in that Country, whereby the pore Christians that inhabit therein, are glad to marry their daughters at twelue yeares of age, vnto Christians, lest the Turkes should rauish them, and to conclude, there is not that sinne in the world, but it is vsed there amongst those Infidels that now inhabit therein,

and

and yet it is called Terra Sancta, & in the Arabian tung Cuthea, which is the holy Land, bearing the name only and no more: for all holinesse is cleane banished from thence by those theeues, filthy Turkes & Infidels that inhabit the same: and hauing my certificate sealed by ye Quadrian, and a letter deliuered vnto me, to shew that I had washed my selfe in the riuer of Iordan, I departed from Ierusalem, in the company of the Moore, that holpe to get me out of prison, leauing Maister Edward Abot, Ieffery Kerbie, Maister Iohn Elken, Iasper Tymne, and Maister Beadle the Preacher (whom I met there by chaunce, not knowing of their comming) behinde me in Ierusalem, and which grieued me most, the Gentleman of Middle-burrow called Maister Iohn Burrell, that I met withall at Grand Cayro, that had borne me company from thence to Ierusalem, forsoke me there, and stayed also in Ierusalem with the other fiue Englishmen, and so I was left alone to the mercy of my Moore that kept me company, and neuer left me till I came to Grand Cayro. Now what hapned vnto me in my traueling from Ierusalem to Cayro, and from thence to Alexandria, where my ship lay, I will hereafter declare.

Departing from Ierusalem, we got safely to Rama, and from thence went to Astalon, and so to Gaza, that lyeth vpon the borders of the desarts of Arabia: at one of those two places I hoped to haue some passage by water, either to Alexandria or to Damietta, but fayling thereof, I was in a maze & knew not what to do, whether I were best to go back againe to Ierusalem, or to put my selfe desperately into ye hands of the wild Arabians, to be by them conducted to Grand Cayro: one of those two courses I must of force take, so there was no hope of passage, and yet I had another hope, but to no end, which was that I should find passage at

E   Ioppa

Ioppa, and for that cause I stayed at Gaza, and sent my Moore to Ioppa to seeke for passage, but their was none to be had. At last considering with my selfe that my haste into Aegipt was great, for I had left my man Waldred in Cayro with my stocke of 1200. poundes, and my ship lay in the Road of Alexndria, with sixty men in her, & whether they would depart without me or no I knew not, for that, when I went from them to goe vp the riuer of Nilus to Cayro. I had no intent to goe for Ierusalem, my businesse standing at that point, I was forced to this extremity, to make away al the mony I had about me, and to put my selfe into the handes of two wilde Arabians, that vndertooke to carrie me and my Moore (without whom I durst not goe) to the Cittie of Cayro in foure dayes, if I would pay them 24. Sultans of gold: when I came to the Materia neere to Cayro, and vpon that condition they would deliuer me safely there, otherwise they said that they would carry me prisoner with them, or else cut my throate: And so agreeing with them by my Moore that spake for me, and with all warranted me to goe safely, swearing that he would not leaue me by any meanes: ye two wild Arabiās prouided vs two god Dromidories for vs to ride on. I and the Moore riding before, and the Arabians behinde vs, two vpon each Dromidorie, and so departed from Gaza about two of the clock in the afternoone, and rode a hard pace: those kind of beastes going so hard, that within foure houres I was so weary that I desired them to suffer me to light downe to rest me, which we did about six of the clocke in the euening, and being alighten, the Arabians tyed the Dromidories two forefeet together as their manner is, making them kneele downe: which done, we sat downe to eate a few raisins and Bisket, such as we caryed in our Alforges but in the meane time one of our Dromidories brake his strings, being but a small peece of a basell, and ranne ran backe againe towards Gaza, whereupon one of the theeues tooke the other Dromidorie, and made after him, vntill both he and the other, that brake loose and ran away, were both out of our sight: then the other Arabian that stayed behinde with vs, ranne after them, and we were left alone in the Wilde Desarts of Arabia: at last, night approaching and both our guides and Dromidories being gone, wee were both in no small feare, what would become of vs, in which case, leauing my More with my Alforyes (wherein we carryed our victualles (I went vp to the toppe of a sandy hill, not farre from thence, to see if I could espie our two Theeues, but I was no soner vppon the toppe of the Hill, but I sawe foure Wilde Arabians come running towards me, from the other side of the Sandy Hill, which I perceiuing, ranne in great haste to my More, yet I could not runne so fast, but one of the Theeues was at my heeles, and drawing out his sword, bad my More deliuer me vnto him, but the More made him answeare and bad him search me (for he knew well that I had nothing about me worth any thing onely my haire cloth Coate) and saide further vnto him, this Guaire (which is as much to say as vnbeleeuer) is to be conducted to Cayro in foure dayes by two of your companions, and therewith named them vnto him, whereunto they all made answeare and saide, that if it were true, they would doe me no hurte, but if their companions came not againe with their Dromidories, then they would carry vs away with them, but within two houres after in the night time, my two Arabians came againe with their Dromidories, and then they were all fellow theeues. And we gaue them a few raisins and a little water, & so departed, and the fourth day at night we came to a place where the Arabians had Tents, and there they gaue me some Camels milke, and beheld me

E 2　　　　　so

so earnestly, as if they had neuer sene a white man before: from thence wee departed, and the next night wee came to Salhia, where being sore shakē in my body (notwithstanding I was rolled with rollers) I was constrained to giue ouer my Dromidories, & to get horses which they procured there of some of their acquaintance: this Dromidorie is a kinde of beast like vnto a Camel, but it hath a lesser head and a very small neck, but his legges are as long, and there is no more difference betwéene a Camell and a Dromidory, then there is betwéene a Masty-Dog and Grey-hound: those beastes eate but little and drinke lesse, for they dranke not as long as I was with them, and it is said that they will not drink in eight or ten dayes together, but cannot abstaine so long from meate. And by this you may sée that I was as far in foure dayes, as I was going in twelue dayes before: I thinke a good horse will run as fast, but not continue it: their pace is a reaching trot, but very hard and quicke. From the edge of Salhia which is vpon the east side of Gozan, I toke horse, but the reason why the Arabians did graunt to get me horses, was not because they pittied me for my wearinesse, but for that they durst not go any néerer to the inhabited countrie with their Dromidories, & there one of them stayed, & the other went with me to Materia, from whence I sent my Moore to Cayro to fetch me their hyer, and there I paid them that let me the horses, fire péeces of gold, and gaue the two wilde Arabians 24. péeces of golde, and therewith they deliuered me in safetie into the custodie of my Moore, within thrée miles of the Citie Cayro, where I was welcomed by the Consull and others there resident, and there I paid my honest Moore fiue péeces of gold, and bought diuers prouisions for him to furnish him in his iourney to Mecha, in which iourney as he returned againe, he dyed.

In Cayro I staied two daies, and the seauenth night
after

after I came to Bullac, and there tooke boate, & in three daies I got downe the riuer of Nilus to Roffetta, and there taking horse with a Ianisarie, I fell into greater danger then any I had during my iourney, for that betweene that towne, and Alexandria, there were diuers great Ianisaries that came from Constantinople, that were newly Landed at Alexandria, who hauing tyred their Horses, would haue taken our two Mules from vs, which my Ianisarie refused them, and therewith drew out his sword, and they to be reuenged came running to take mee, and hauing laide hands vppon me, foure of them beate me cruelly, and draue me to the passage that was hard by, and there would haue killed me. which my Ianisarie perceiuing, and seeing that nothing could appease the but our two Mules; after he had bin sore wounded, he deliuered them vnto the other Ianisaries, or else I had there bin slaine, after my long and wearie iourny, being within fiue miles of my ship, that lay in the Rode at Alexandria, and so he being sore wounded and I wel beaten, at last we got to the gates of Alexandria, but it was so late that we could not get in, but were forced to stay al y night (til morning) vpon the hard stones, & in the morning I got aborde of my ship, when I had bin from it fiftie daies. And so I ended my Pilgrimage.

FINIS.

Lightning Source UK Ltd.
Milton Keynes UK
11 April 2011

170708UK00005B/28/P